Hooligans

Also by Lillian Nećakov

The Bone Broker (Mansfield Press, 2007)
Polaroids (Coach House Press, 1998)
Hat Trick (Exile Editions, 1998)
The Sickbed of Dogs (Wolsak & Wynn, 1989)
Listen (Pink Dog Press, 1988)
A Cowboy in Hamburg (Surrealist Poets' Gardening Assoc., 1985)
And Crunch (Proper Tales Press, 1982)

Hooligans

Lillian Nećakov

Nećakov [signature]

For "Boneshaking" check page 27.

For Kent

Mansfield Press

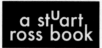

Copyright © Lillian Nećakov 2011
All Rights Reserved
Printed in Canada

Library and Archives Canada Cataloguing in Publication

Nećakov, Lillian, 1960-
    Hooligans / Lillian Nećakov.

Poems.
ISBN 978-1-894469-58-6

    I. Title.

PS8577.E33H66 2011   C811'.54   C2011-906357-3

Editor for the Press: Stuart Ross
Design: Denis De Klerck
Typesetting: Stuart Ross
Cover Illustrations: Shutterstock
Author Photo: Andrew Avalos

The publication of *Hooligans* has been generously supported by the Canada Council for the Arts and the Ontario Arts Council.

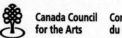

Mansfield Press Inc.
25 Mansfield Avenue, Toronto, Ontario, Canada M6J 2A9
Publisher: Denis De Klerck
www.mansfieldpress.net

"I fear those big words which make us so unhappy"

James Joyce

Contents

The Chronologist / 9
Secret Hanging / 10
Murder by Hunger / 12
Ice in Spain / 14
Death Gutter / 15
The Dalai Lama Test / 16
Dancing Goats / 18
Hurricane / 19
Bus Trip #1 / 20
F=*ma* / 21
Real Dogs / 23
Obliquity of the Ecliptic / 24
The Wedding / 25
Larks / 26
Boneshaker / 27
Forgetting Jesus / 28
Hooligans / 29
The Dictaphone at Work / 30
Zero Day / 31
Dear Romeo / 33
Night Writing / 35
Arm Wrestling in November / 38
Why / 39
The Burning Man / 40
Tribunal del Santo Oficio de la Inquisición / 42
Symptoms / 43
Strolling on Borrowed Ankles / 44
A Percentage of Joy / 45
The Butterfly Lovers / 46
Me and Buddha in High Park / 47

Skating to America / 48
Mathematics / 50
Remembrance Day / 52
The Gene Pool / 53
Kandinsky Highway / 54
Bus Trip #2 / 56
Hermetics / 57
The Walking Debt / 58
Jones / 59
HeLa / 60
Bird Talking / 62
Shipwrecked / 63
The Square / 65
What We Lost / 66
On the Fifth Day of Rain / 67
Charm Bird / 68
The Sickness We Speak / 69
The Kid Is Lost / 70
Everything You Know Is Not True / 71
A Guide to Understanding Graphology / 72
That Monkey Is Dead / 73

The Chronologist

What I aim to say is
my entire life could fit into one shoe
but what comes out is:

I need an ampersand
I like reading the periodic table
neither the stick nor the tree is mine
nothing was ever a consequence
not even the inability to breathe
I am a papier mâché doll
raining tears in a summer temple
the word "factory" is my favourite
libraries fear my teeth
parking meters are sacred
I will never be a great Canadian poet
they will never seat us in the sun
I am glad your soul is drifting
into the evening coolness
a lonely autumn grips my heart
you can't count on me
I have no faith
tomorrow is too soon
I am a coward
I failed chemistry
Ornette Coleman broke my heart.

Secret Hanging

On the balcony of my mother's house
pumpkins sprout stars
to guide me back to her arms
but the secret I carry under my toenails
outgrows each seed planted
in this aviary full of knees and blindness
I am as dangerous as a burst fire hydrant
they tell me

I had wings once
darker than a crow's
and stronger than an eagle's
until cannibalized by bald fingers

I covet laughter
curl into myself like a dried tongue
I hear the backwash current of the drowning machine
every day of every year
outside my window
I see the noose calm as poison
beautiful as linen
hung from the maypole
I am innocent of everything
but wanting

there are drops of water on the fence outside
I move my lips
I have a mother, a dead sister, a father
I holler muteness down the hill
they awaken

to deafness
I see the hangman
squeezing happiness into his eyes
I have lips
there is thirst.

Murder by Hunger

Something happened
and a bunch of people died
a whole country
body count equalling an ant colony

he gets out of his car as if to take a leak
but really it is random
he needs a place to rest his head
understand his mother's grief
finger the eternal loneliness

somewhere baseballs multiply in factories
music billows out of smoke stacks
his mouth is full of broken teeth

Ma Rainey is belting out Article 58
the long hours of his childhood
string together
to form a rope of ornamental lights
the colour of orchids

from across the tundra he hears
his mother's voice saying
pull up your socks, Joseph
and he sleeps on

something happened
and people died
the spit and sizzle of electrical wires
wakes him

fragments of strangers' prayers stuck to his skin
he lifts himself to his feet
don't look back
he walks and he walks and he walks
and he doesn't stop.

Ice in Spain

The woman in the photograph
cremated her husband
only yesterday
while the snow falls in Harlem
and here
like cherry blossoms
of sadness
scars from a suffering sky
awkward little swallows
plump notes
piano peace
settling over strands of frozen hair
on a street without ploughs.

Death Gutter

I have dangerous questions
about water and atom smashers
calipers
New Orleans
about why the synapses in my brain
diffuse light and chronicle the milky way
while yours, insignificant and odious
fizzle and wane like soggy matches

the bomb shelters and machine guns of our childhood
are the same lies they use today
only the paint is leadless
less toxic
less obvious

I have dangerous sadness
about your buildings
those giant cadavers filled with wires
ears, bones, jaws
but no real language

I have dangerous lips
to press to your forehead
under different circumstances
different skies.

The Dalai Lama Test

"In the words of the ancients, one should make his decisions
within the space of seven breaths."
— Hagakure, *The Book of the Samurai*

They asked him for his soul
and he pointed to the sky
they asked him to draw the antlers of a deer
and he made them dream of magnificent beasts
when they asked him to name the constellations
he signed the names so brilliantly
they thought they had heard him reciting
they asked him to run like the wind
and he shook the leaves off a nearby tree
they asked him to bleed
and he filled their cupped hands
with warm saltless tears
they asked him to sing the future and the past
he closed his eyes and opened his mouth
radiant plumes of colour escaped

only the wind howled

while soul boy lay mute on the drying dirt
they asked
and he did not hear
his mother brushed away tears
her heart full of milk and a thousand winds
her son would remain anonymous
insufficient, wrong, broken

her joy fused with the clouds
and she lifted her boy into her arms
brushing his misshapen ears
with her lips
she whispered

now
you will travel with the other children on the school bus
and I will name you...

Dancing Goats

I read a book about an Ethiopian goat herder,
a bunch of bright red berries
and what happened to the goats
when they chewed the berries
I told you this was the story of coffee
in the cold night
with Abyssinian fingers tapping against my spine
I remembered to tell you everything
I was supposed to

you mixed kindness with lemon seeds
with which to perfume the snow
just that once
the tiny details
reflected in your eyes
conquered kingdoms and beasts alike

the sky hung from a sliver of broken bone.

Hurricane

On a languid August day
I pedalled my bicycle down Runnymede Road
and saw Hurricane Carter
getting out of a black Mercedes Benz

the light was already changing
from open windows drifted
the buttery rhythms of Dexter Gordon
shadows were slower and longer
summer would soon be
only a remarkable wave of nostalgia

without a sound or wave
I pedalled on
into the foreseeable shenanigans of autumn.

Bus Trip #1

There is a girl crying on the bus
I want to hold her hand
so she can feel the rope-like scars
running across my skin
from the time I set myself on fire
when my mother was dying

instead I look out the window
at a city gone wrong.

F=*m*a

I told you I was a verb
when really I am just a semicolon
an afterthought

with each mathematical dilemma
my brain performs contortions
"Force equals mass times acceleration"
classroom simplicity

walking past the Tran Tran Bakery
I see Archimedes
but it is just the wind
forces acting on the body
Newton's second law
along St. Clair Avenue
with windows full of scheming oranges
and I can't remember the last time I felt the sun

moving through the grooves of memory
to some distant Big Bill Broonzy beat
ruminating theorems
curved genius along the cracked pavement
walk
just walk
unlock the door
go to work
and know
that your life would have turned out simpler
if Wilbur and Orville were your childhood friends
that if you hadn't spent your time boxing Gordie Robson

you would know co-efficiency, density, velocity
the lift equation

know too that if Sonny Terry and Brownie McGhee
had not conspired to map your dreams
you would not have fallen in love
with David McFadden's *Gypsy Guitar*
Pi would only amount to 3
the universe would be shapeless
a deflated cow's belly
punctuated by a kaleidoscope
filled with colourless glass.

Real Dogs

the shovels are put away
for another year
there is nothing to trip over
dogs twitch and scramble
clawing
towards
then under
then past the *Jesus Saves* sign

I run after them
hollering
my book bag flailing in the sunlight
down this ugly street

once there were icebergs here
now fragments of birds' nests
dot the sidewalk in warning
a rusty barbecue
whistles in the wind
everyone is sorry
everyone is frightened

static fills my ears
this is a natural disaster
time is *so* furious with us
there will be no foot stomping
no final jig
only a single flea dancing across a strand of hair
but what do they know
they are just stupid dogs.

Obliquity of the Ecliptic

The trees sway
despite the exodus of birds
haunted by music
somewhere a roomful of people listens
to what my footsteps might sound like
nothing slips off the earth
not dog carcasses
spent bombs
adagios
nor bus conductors
not a drop of us spills
from this tilted planet
23.44° is not enough to erase
the smell and sound of kill.

The Wedding

There is a town in Ontario
that smells of sulphur
he knows this because
he travelled there once
for a wedding

he sat on the edge of a bed
in a motel room
remembered he had left his speech
in a hut somewhere next to a forgotten tricycle
opened his mouth
and a single ornament spilled into his empty hands

he fixed his tie
moved to the windowsill
in shoes crisp and black as a carpet beetle
placing his palms against a windowsill
sprinkled with dead flies
like giant poppy seeds
or the black letters his father taught him
to trace
he wished a wish so secret
it could only be heard by a stevedore
an entire country away.

Larks

When my mother was dying
it wasn't a child's place to ask how or why
so my brother and I stood, quiet against the dark mahogany
trying not to be noticed
at the same time hoping
someone would recognize the curious electricity in our eyes

after that
there were nights and stories and photographs
but not of her
it was as though someone else had given birth to us
and we saw her face only in dreams

we watched cartoons
and *Star Trek* and walked to school with all the other children

but we were unkempt and hollow
hearts filled with broken teeth
lost as the larks we would find on our porch
and the voice that sang us to sleep at nights was our own

as we grew and outgrew each other
we remained moored in our love of the stars and planets
an invisible ribbon of laughter
tethered us to the night skies
orchestrating a happiness
felt only on occasion
when our spinning lamp would rotate and flutter
and for a split second her face would light up
the dark corners of our room.

Boneshaker

His lips are coated with rust
he can taste the taste of falling in love
he follows the dirt road to the smoke stacks
beardless, he carries a folksong
he is swift, can feel the atoms flickering through his body
he hears the cadence of desolation
and his bones shifting like tectonic plates
she waves to him from a distance
he spins and pedals
legs of oak
ankles of bone
repeating
the word
opposite
the word opposite
to love.

Forgetting Jesus

There are people who say
we are angry
but that is not true
we are just afraid
gloomy
we don't know
what lies inside the shell of an oyster
we are not as clever as the farmers
who can find the vocabulary of the sky
in a nest full of robin's eggs.

Hooligans

There was a man
who once dragged a tugboat
over a mountain
I believe he dreamt of penitentiaries
filled with tiny black beetles
bustling up and down the anemic plaster
like notes across sheet music conducting themselves
as wondrous as Mahler's *Titan*
as dark as Lou Reed

the man was the son of another man
who was a tinker

sometimes he would stand by the pylons for hours
waiting for what he had done to be undone
other times he travelled to exotic destinations
in his head
his compass always drawing him home

this man actually ate his shoe
while following the arc of a falling tree
when he was little
his mother called him
schatzi and *liebe*
I wish I was this man
when *we* were little
my mother called us hooligans.

The Dictaphone at Work

they handed him the machine
at first he spoke delicately
about gulags, cathedrals, castles
nothing of scientific interest
only a detailed description
of the aberrant map emblazoned
across his shoulders

this represents years
and this
the possibility of love

they asked him to speak up
evaporate language
change the world
explain
the history of his eyes
he was saddened
by this last request
feeling the warm wood
under his bare skin
he let out a howl
causing the machine to hiss and sizzle
to the absence of music
and for all eyes
he pointed

this represents the pebbles they made me swallow
and this
the hatred growing from nothing.

Zero Day

In a place where there is no milk
he blinks
what the rat told him
is true
black *is* the queen of colours

there is a bend in the road
where the empty shell of his brother lies
blanched and drying
under an alabaster sun
and he says it doesn't matter
but it is anchored
in his mind
"zeru"
a brother with frosted eyelashes
transparent
through the seasons
ghost
a pearl
pressed against the blackness
of their mother

the breeze undoes him
lips cracked
he approaches the edge
his chest fills with the sounds of the cellist
heard only once
pride comes in waves
as he lifts the little shell to *his* lips

the first drop is metallic
followed by sweetness
tears find their way into him
there is no cure
for snow in the blood
his brother is gone
taken
for his bird-like limbs
which now lay sleeping at the bottom of a volcano

mediators stomp
the dirt complies
bells jingle
bringing on the ecstasy
he watches as the spirit of zeru rides on their shoulders
and wishes his skin was not king.

Dear Romeo

It is October 7th and I am sad

a strange little man jumped in front of a subway car
the other day

I am confronted with wizened flowers
and smudged eulogies
as I enter the High Park station

the sun is warm and persistent
the man at the post office—black as tar—
smiles at me
as if to say
"such things happen"

today
I think of you
as I run my fingers along
the cool metal of my bicycle
what did you tell the allies when they came?
could they see
the pictures in your head?
whatever you did is alright
I am only angry with you
because of what you saw
and because you then told me

I carried your book with me through three seasons
like an uncharted melody
—that moment during childhood
when you realize the meaning

of a very small word
and suddenly
where happiness was once an entire hemisphere
you find yourself standing on only an inch or two of possibility—

I have to tell you
David McFadden wrote a whole book of poems
called *Why Are You So Sad?*
he is a sad Canadian like you and me
his heart is not bent though
he knows how to stop the chaos

I run for miles
to outrun my own self
my footprints
your insomnia
the hate
right
left
right
invisible rhythms of breath
something resembling peace
then beats and drumming
and bullets
pounding and machetes
last breaths

this is the thirty-fourth letter I have written you
and never sent
I am sad, Romeo.

Night Writing

for Gilbert Tuhabonye

Gilbert was not born a gazelle
the voice he knows best tells him this
"run" it says
he complies
his boundless strides spill into the night
he feels the pulse of Songa
the cadence of his father's words
the roughness of his mother's fingers
he pilfers a thought
and for a brief moment is solitary

there is a fork in the road
he *is* a consequence
he *cannot* outrun his cauterized body
the hours, seconds, nanoseconds
spent trying to force his tongue to prayer
cannot
outrun the inferno that ached for him
the giant umbrella of bodies
he wept under
and can still feel on cool autumn evenings

the route he takes determines
in what sequence the memories will attack
his arms pump, propel him further
from the schoolhouse
he *feels* nothing
remembers everything

the drumming in his ears
and the stench remind him
he is alive

this fork takes him to the river
safe
his lips touch the water
silence is broken
by the sizzling of his own skin
being extinguished

Gilbert takes a fine picture
the photographer is pleased
she is allowed to capture the mottled scars
like night writing
the code that distinguishes him
from every other man
that tells his story without punctuation
or pause
21 raised dots that spell out his name
in any language

she runs her camera along his eroded skin
wondering what evil sired
this landscape

this road
leads to something akin to sleep
where fire does not *lick*
it engraves
scorches
ignites
scalds
remembers

there are sixty-four permutations in braille
all stating
Gilbert is a gazelle.

Arm Wrestling in November

So, spring has busted in on us
an arm wrestle determining the outcome
of this once-in-the-history-of-time
November day

there are no bombs or shells
helicopters or mortars
nothing of consequence is going on
but even this fragmented little road remembers

under the streetcar tracks skeletons of lilac and hibiscus roots
lie in wait
fault lines

this morning
the contours of your perfect face as you slept
reminded me of the map of our failing universe
—*those tiny specks not yet marred by fate or fury*—
as I left, I whispered to you as all good mothers do
and you did not stir.

Why

Because my dog said so
and because the geese are evil
because I know a one-legged man
and because Leiban spit in my face
because the Celtics lost
and I hate mushrooms
because I keep your dried-up umbilical cord in my jewellery box
and because there is a tree in my living room
because you call me a "lawn chair"
and move across my shadow like an eclipse
because your brother died
and mine didn't
because I hate love stories
and because Jim never calls me
because I sometimes write shitty poems
and because my daughter is a lamppost
because I once kissed a boy in the drive-in cinema
and because my father wears a girdle on sweltering days
because my step-mother has plastic hips
and because you made me listen to Gustav Mahler
when I told you repeatedly I hate Mahler
because my legs are scarred
and I know who did it
because ten minutes is a hell of a long time
when someone is holding a gun to your head.

The Burning Man

All clocks are zeroed once he kneels
the shadows are loose and grave
maps of pain change his body
prepare his bones
to twist
oxidize and etch themselves in the pavement

he makes a wish
I don't hear it or see it
but there is something in the ferocity
of stillness
he is laden
not with regret
the approaching night gathers armloads of hope

where the hell did this photograph find me?
what bartering will it take to erase
the miserable, hellish record, once I have closed the book
or turned the page?

I am distracted
by the wind chimes
then I am stupid
I need to see it again
the soldier looking for a light
cigarette hanging from indifferent lips
one order of magnitude from now
the monk is lit on fire
by his own hands
no one minds

the sidewalk accommodates the flaming soloist
the sky is good
the mind is a funny thing
I think of knitting needles
enamel tapping against enamel

another order of magnitude from now
a well-intentioned Mississippian could have stumbled upon this scene
as easily as I did
his heart would have shrunken a size or two
and when he closed his eyes at night
seven monks would have evaporated
into the dawn.

Tribunal del Santo Oficio de la Inquisición

Picture your boyfriend as a pile of rocks
1000 volts of electricity shooting through him
what is your instinct now?
and the gymnastics of your mind?
are petals dropping somewhere?

Symptoms

When you begin with a verb
everything else is downhill
falsehoods carry you
until you reach the cupola and find
no throne of gold
just a recurring obsession punctuated
by a dog's head on a broomstick

the alchemy of love is so arbitrary
it makes your forehead ache

the coroner oils his gurney
while the soothsayers rock you
to sleep and beyond

when you end with a verb
traffic begins to stop
a boomerang by the side of the road
and raging love.

Strolling on Borrowed Ankles

Tapping stones together means
you are not a couch potato
memories divide themselves
into other memories
atoms of memory
memory of atoms
the yellow of beauty
the groan of wood under your boots
along the boardwalk
echoing across the Thursday lake
to where Andy can feel your heart
unravelling like a giant spool
miles away from your garage
that once meant something to you
but for now there are more amusing things
like parks encased in parks
and ice on your mind
layers of jutting hope along the shore
a discarded subway token
your smile reminiscent of chickens; a proton
positively charged
a streetcar full of moon
quieter hours
and a curb
waiting to congratulate you
while you rest your borrowed ankles.

A Percentage of Joy

The guy in the swimming pool said
lightning
it was lightning
we should all get out
he was sober
so we believed him
but there were better stories
remember?

like the time
they x-rayed his bones
looking for diseases
fissures
barnacles
joy
and found only a lung
a comma
and a small shadow
awaiting its bloom.

The Butterfly Lovers

When the black ladies stop singing
we put on our shirtsleeves
and listen to the grotesque silence
of the factory wall

ossuaries full of butterflies
signal summer's end
pools of oil carrying our reflections
settle in front of mailboxes
around the world
while the fluttering and stutter
of resplendent wings desists.

Me and Buddha in High Park

First day of spring
and plus and plus the geese
with small trepidation
against the gruesome fish
vintage laughter
across a pond.

Skating to America

for David McFadden on his 70th birthday

I told you
we could skate clear across
when the lake was frozen
and all the drops of water welded together
I lied
because I could see your heart pounding
like a sparrow's
in your tiny chest
and I couldn't
disappoint you
not yet

I told you the sun had teeth
despite its brilliance
I told you I was black on the inside
and that in our house
there was a room for every emotion
I climbed to the roof and riffed you to sleep
with delicate dulcet lies
because you were still unaware
of the circumference of a stranger
because I couldn't
not yet

I told you lies squared
and more
but the truest thing I told you
was about a man named David

who drove around the entire lake
in his little red car
and that if you strung all his words together
and followed them
like a procession
they would weave you through radiant angles
on your journey
his words would rip a hole in the night
to reveal a sequence of fossils
skating you all the way to America
you would be cageless
if you felt his voice
sliding across your lips
and this life would not be a mistake.

Mathematics

Galileo shouts at the pope and the church
and all the holy men
in the complaining house
that the moon is not smooth

if I believed in reincarnation I'd swear
he had come back as Mos Def
it would be the most elegant of dictums
and no matter how many numbers they twisted and conjoined
they could never disprove it

but I only believe in the weathervane I see
the blindness that won't lay off
that steals the architecture of their step
as they follow the accordion's warble
on legs as weak as tassels

the universe is expanding
there is a precise numerical rhyme
that can explain the sun
I am not dreaming
the rings of Saturn are engraved with
the laws and stories of cosmology
Galileo knew and Copernicus before him
that if you ran your fingers across these grooves
god would cease to exist

and so at night
I sing to them about
fluid dynamics, chaos theory and differential equations
hoping that in sleep
they will conjure
an algorithm
to replace the weight of the host on their tongues.

Remembrance Day

He was an orphan
before he was a widower
under the fig tree
his shadow wore a crown
girls in sandals
followed him without destination
approximating
wilting daffodils
under a raging sun

this was before
we knew him as our father
before his DNA clung to the discreet recesses of ourselves
before the smell of everyone he has lost
before it was too late for a different syntax
before turning back clocks
before we were his quagmire
before the vagaries of weather
before we were the sole occupants of his fears
before she left him nothing but her skeleton
in a fortress filled with waning light.

The Gene Pool

The drunken streetcar
of my father's dreams
visits me always on yesterdays
where I am the custodian of insomnia.

Kandinsky Highway

We talk about revolutions we didn't belong to
or couldn't
moving east
along a road that has a twin

there is the smell of apple and remarkably
a mutation:
in the back seat sits
the shell of a giant turtle
covered in lithographs chronicling
our abandoned friendship
whispering
"are we there yet"

while the brain adjusts itself to the nuances of fading light
we keep existing
along a corridor of dismantled shops, faded awnings
broken antennas
there is a brief possibility that our thoughts will leap onto the asphalt
joining the paint strips that loiter
in the twilight of this passing day
until you tell me we are on the Kandinsky highway
and I raise my eyes
to this uncertain gift

apparently we arrive
heaps of sadness wrapped in limestone and stained glass
"this is my town—was my town"
slips off your tongue

as easily as a blossom drifting from its branch
how are we here
in a different city
with the same thoughts
the same wind blowing
the same carp in the same lake
that we never finished driving around
how are we here
under this sky so much like a tar pit
with stars settled into its inkiness
shrapnel
illuminating our invasion of the jail keeper's turf

fishing rods poised
we dip into this chestnut night
foliage cascading around us
poachers of lexicon.

Bus Trip #2

There is no one on the bus
the sun has wedged itself
between the ribcages
of clouds
a generous helping of fists
propels me off my actual feet
an image of steaming nostrils
escorts me
as my cheek collides with the sidewalk.

Hermetics

The intention of pigeons
is to outlive us
to weather the tourists and wires and tubes
the fight and the fall, the postmen
and the circus
their plan is to gorge
on the dispatches
spilling from our books
and leave no evidence
of cruel bodies
governed
only by gravity.

The Walking Debt

The man behind the altar said
I was a mermaid
my door is open
sang the pale girl next to me
a griffin counted
on his talons
the number of miles
we needed to walk

if this was the church
the adulation
—shoulders slouched
like old playing cards
fingering fish braided into prayer ropes—
where was the absolution

wait for the birds
sang the choir
and no angels arrived
a hundred dark judgments fluttered
out of my incision
the distance we must walk
is in direct proportion to our trespass
and the cimmerian graffiti
scored across our afternoons.

Jones

Decades later
an infernal rooftop on college street
imagines it is a pelican

from its wings
laughter slides into the streetcar tracks
making all the lunchboxes cheer.

HeLa

The empire state building is bursting at its seams
ebony cells quiver
breed
and divide
into cyan weeds
tiny nuances of life
vessels of sorrow and genius
where you begin and I end

leagues from here
embraced by the warm southern dirt
under tobacco leaves the size of a vulture's wing
her bones rest quietly
shifting with time
and weather

her legacy festers
under the chewed fingernails of scientists
a malignant stolen treasure
bearing fruit
upon fruit
until the atmosphere
heavies, ripens
and must weep

her hair was once so pretty
all of Africa smiled
before the knot
that tightened with each step
and drained the body of its will

until there was no more flow
or cadence
until her blood stopped shuttling oxygen
until day closed his eyes on her face

syringes filled with
bits of taut muscle
that once wrapped itself around her heart
now long gone
wash up on distant shores
to watch over twisted limbs
and cure the fever
in cities gone blind

her grace is spread across this earth
like coral
acrobats fling themselves at the moon
in search of her headstone
blossoming forgiveness
on the coloured side.

Bird Talking

There is a fishery in Newfoundland where I've never been
and always remembered

a place where a girl
is singing
under a sky brimming with milk-filled clouds
during moonlight
when the gathering of memories
collapses day into night

a place where
a blackbird will weave you a new skin
and angle your heart
into the fading light of the harbour
to speak of love
and kings that never die

you come and go with promises
chestnut eyes filled with rain
and a sandstorm collecting in your chest

close your mouth
your eyes
let slip the mist from your shoulders
I will hold you this once
under uncharted skies
a bucketful of angel bones
dancing you to sleep.

Shipwrecked

for Jim

Below the equator
a man named Nicanor Parra
sleeps under a blazing meteor
I fear his shoes might be full of meaning

he was once younger than I am now
his enzymes curing and reshaping the disease of language
until he was able to utter
the nuances of the universe like a caged bird
dreaming of flight

across the pond I hear the geese
remembering Chilean nights
flecked with merken and fractals
nights set on fire by the audacity of numbers
and the hand of a poet
waving his spirit across the boulevards of summer

you step into the ocean
in search of a house with broken windows
spilling laughter-filled stones into the meandering streets
until the wind—like an ugly dog—
threatens your escape
and you are shipwrecked
somewhere between snow and imagination

in your pocket
the horizon weeps against your fingers
all the years spent searching for his voice
are now silent

the distance is immense
and so
each night I will sing you his name
until his grace finds you
and shields you from the darkness
of the northern hemisphere.

The Square

The first line of defense is to run
but when the fragile crown you are carrying
slips between your fingers like silk
and you fall to your knees in the square
lost in a mob of legs
the click and clack
of heels against stone
gravity lures you
to rest your head as if listening for a train
that will never come
to wait for a sun
that has forgotten how to sail
stains of colour dance past you
elbows and wind spirit you away
and click
and
clack
the rifles sing metal songs
chambered rounds
clack
the sky is thick with thrush
waiting for ether
for the voice of memory on swimsuited days
by the sea
by train
by whatever means
to swallow the kiss and sleep
to rest your head on one day as smooth as mink
as mundane as syrup
but there are always anchors.

What We Lost

The cow the antlers our voice
the silence our shoes the compass
the afternoon the ink the meridian

then
between pageless books and cracking farms
in the museums of rain
rusty anvils
will cleave our story
like a patient storm
perched in the heart of a dreaming bird.

On the Fifth Day of Rain

The emperor shakes his head
in the immeasurable thickness of our brains
we have failed
we did not stroll beside him in the companionship of sunlight
we did not admire the letters rippling his tongue
nor did we fetch the morning sky for him
to fold into tiny feet
that would carry us away from this epileptic trajectory

the emperor closes his eyes
drops a shoe
a great migration of birds
swoops over us
the wristwatches of my life
are drowning.

Charm Bird

O'clock on the ticker this far
north the train is on its leaving
acronychal bird trills slice through wheat
carving daylight off the horizon
draping darkness around our shoulders
the road curves only so much before you arrive at winter
where the shutting of windows is a season

hurry off the tractor
one last time
abandon yourself to the cracked fingers of summer
brushing against your neck.

The Sickness We Speak

In the dream we know
my legs are glass

and all the fish melt
into the malachite sea

when the thermometer is broken
the sun dial is a lie

and the salt on our lips
is the sorrow of a small boy

in the shed behind her house
my tonsils rattle

and the metronome imagines itself
a castanet

if the stones we skip are perfect
the sun will always be our anchor

if you die
in my dream

your mouth will find me
in waking.

The Kid Is Lost

The summer I got burnt by the sun Grace's husband Bud died
and we all went to the funeral home on the Danforth
it seemed we had come upon a new town
the summer storm cracked against our knuckles
cooling the fire in my skin
leaving us with nothing but vowels and rocks in our throats
we stood cemented, obedient with bare legs
like cows leaning into one another for comfort against the sky
a fabric of cells and skin
terrified of the watchmaker
who set all watches to the rhythm of obituary pages
feeling our own bodies alive and dripping with rain
flawless in youth
afraid of seeming too eager
knees buckling under too little wisdom
under hearts laid horizontal to rest
on a street that belongs to someone else
and from across the way laughter
giving us an excuse to exhale all the tragedy
we swayed and faltered under the glances of strangers
nitrogen infused finger touching finger
vertices patterned into the beginning
of the end of us together
and a paper boy whistled as long and clear as a reflection
"the kid is lost" we figured
and stood so sharply against that idea.

Everything You Know Is Not True

The mother who carried you like a whisper
on her tongue
is now just a tiny gathering of foam
drifting out to sea

the balconies once held up by her halo
lie shattered across the sidewalk

you remember a house
heaving shoulders
a mattress
more importantly
telegraphs
delivered like eggs at the doorstep

the father whose voice tempered
the steps of your journey
is a beautiful dog
gliding peacefully through the streets
in search of fire hydrants

when you die
someone will take your spot in the sun
and brave lies
will grow out of that moment
filling the summer air
like fireflies.

A Guide to Understanding Graphology

The writer does not join his letters
the writer has a puritan streak
the writer is feeling dragged down
likes people, is well organized
dislikes noise and violence
is overwhelmed, meek and a mongrel
the writer's fingerprints are lavishly spread across the girl's body
crime is only an instinct when followed by action
there is chatter in the room
a small zone of difficulty surrounded by police tape
bears the weight of what is on his mind
typical jobs: jockey, apprentice, politician, taxidermist

the writer slants his pen toward the snow filling his cranium

That Monkey Is Dead

They are asking
for a ransom
we get our monkey back
but the sweet smell of mock orange
drifting down the avenue
transcends our notions of guilt and desire

without malice
there is no battle
and we walk away into the gentle night.

Acknowledgements

Earlier versions of some of these poems have appeared in *Exile: the Literary Quarterly*, *This Magazine* and *A Trip Around McFadden*. Thank you to the editors of these publications.

Thank you to Drew, Cinco and Max for finishing the equation; my dear friend Jim Smith for Kandinsky Highway and much more; Richard Huttel for correspondence and inspiration; Denis De Klerck for continuing to believe in my writing.

A special thank you to Stuart Ross for his encouragement and perceptive, intelligent, spot-on editing!

I gratefully acknowledge the support of the Ontario Arts Council.

This book is for Aria—the bravest hooligan I know.

 Lillian Nećakov is the author of a bunch of books of poetry, including *The Bone Broker* (Mansfield Press) and *Hat Trick* (Exile Editions). She runs the Boneshaker Reading Series in Toronto, where she lives with her family.

Other Books from Mansfield Press

Poetry
Stephen Brockwell & Stuart Ross, eds., *Rogue Stimulus: The Stephen Harper Holiday Anthology for a Prorogued Parliament*
Alice Burdick, *Flutter*
Gary Michael Dault, *The Milk of Birds*
Pier Giorgio Di Cicco, *Early Works*
Christopher Doda, *Aesthetics Lesson*
Rishma Dunlop, *Lover Through Departure: New and Selected Poems*
Jason Heroux, *Emergency Hallelujah*
David W. McFadden, *Be Calm, Honey*
Leigh Nash, *Goodbye, Ukulele*
Peter Norman, *At the Gates of the Theme Park*
Natasha Nuhanovic, *Stray Dog Embassy*
Catherine Owen & Joe Rosenblatt, with Karen Moe, *Dog*
Corrado Paina, *Souls in Plain Clothes*
Jim Smith, *Back Off, Assassin! New & Selected Poems*
Robert Earl Stewart, *Campfire Radio Rhapsody*
Carey Toane, *The Crystal Palace*
Priscila Uppal, *Winter Sport: Poems*
Steve Venright, *Floors of Enduring Beauty*

Fiction
Marianne Apostolides, *The Lucky Child*
Kent Nussey, *A Love Supreme*
Marko Sijan, *Mongrel*
Tom Walmsley, *Dog Eat Rat*

Non-Fiction
George Bowering, *How I Wrote Certain of My Books*
Pier Giorgio Di Cicco, *Municipal Mind*
Amy Lavender Harris, *Imagining Toronto*